OHIO

in words and pictures

BY DENNIS B. FRADIN

ILLUSTRATIONS BY ROBERT ULM

Consultant
Dr. Charles A. Isetts
Archives-Manuscript Reference Librarian
The Ohio Historical Society

 CHILDRENS PRESS, CHICAGO

Autumn in Ohio

Library of Congress Cataloging in Publication Data

Fradin, Dennis.
  Ohio in words and pictures.

  SUMMARY: A brief history of the Buckeye state with
a description of its countryside and major cities.
  1. Ohio—History—Juvenile literature. 2. Ohio—
Description and travel—1951—Juvenile literature.
[1. Ohio—History. 2. Ohio—Description and travel]
I. Ulm, Robert. II. Title.
F491.3.F7   977.1   76-46941
ISBN 0-516-03935-0

7 8 9 10 11 12 R 85 84 83

Picture Acknowledgements:
DEPT. OF DEVELOPMENT, COLUMBUS, OHIO—Cover, 25 (right), 29 (top left and right)
DEPT. OF ECONOMIC AND COMMUNITY DEVELOPMENT—7, 10, 14, 16, 25, (left), 29 (bottom left), 31 (bottom), 32 (top right), 32 (left), 35 (right), 35 (left), 43
GREATER CLEVELAND GROWTH ASSOCIATION—20, 21, 22, 27 (bottom)
PHOTO COURTESY GOODYEAR TIRE AND RUBBER CO.—24
DEPT. OF INTERIOR, NATIONAL PARK SERVICE PHOTO BY RICHARD FREAR—27 (top); PHOTO BY TEDD McCANN—33 (top left and right), 37
THE CINCINNATI HISTORICAL SOCIETY—31 (center), 33 (left)
CINCINNATI MAGAZINE—31 (top), 32 (bottom right)

COVER PICTURE: View of Columbus taken with a fisheye lens.

Ohio is an Iroquois (EER • ih • kwoi) Indian word meaning *something great.*

Ohio (oh • HI • oh) is one of the smaller states. Yet seven presidents were born here. The airplane was invented here. Today, Ohio's factories make tires for your car and soap for your bath. Ohio proves that a state—like a person—does not have to be big to be great!

MAMMOTH

Millions of years ago, there were plenty of dinosaurs but no people here. Oceans covered the land. Finally, the water dried. Minerals were left in the ground. This is why Ohio is so rich in coal, salt, oil, and limestone.

The age of the dinosaurs ended. The Ice Age began. During the Ice Age, huge blocks of ice, called *glaciers* (GLAY . shers), moved down from the north. Glaciers covered most of Ohio. They flattened the hills. Finally, the glaciers melted, leaving behind layers of smooth, rich soil. That is why Ohio is a fine place for growing crops.

Near the end of the Ice Age, the first people roamed the land. In 1967 the skeleton of an Ice Age man was found in Ohio. He had only a stone knife to protect his family from saber-toothed tigers and other wild animals.

The first people to build homes here were the
Mound Builders. The Mound Builders hunted and
farmed the land. They built wooden houses and forts.
But they are best known for their earth mounds,
which can still be seen today. Pottery and bones have
been found inside. Several of the mounds are
shaped like huge birds and snakes. Why were the
mounds built? That is still a mystery.

Scientists think the Mound Builders were related to the Indians who came later. Indians lived in Ohio for hundreds of years. They hunted deer and buffalo. They fished in the rivers. They grew crops of corn and tobacco.

Some of the Indian tribes were the Delaware (DELL • ah • ware), Miami (my • AM • ee), Iroquois (EER • ih • kwoi), and Shawnee (SHAW • nee). Some of the great chiefs were Pontiac and Cornstalk, Logan and Little Turtle.

Miamisburg Mound

Serpent Mound

La Salle (la • SAL) is thought to be the first explorer
in Ohio. He explored the area for France from 1669-
1670. Later, people from France came to settle here.
Some traded with friendly Indians.

But the English, who controlled the American colonies, also claimed the land. English traders and settlers came, too.

The French, the Indians, and the English fought over Ohio. England won this war. Now the king of England ruled Ohio—just as he ruled the 13 American colonies in the East.

More settlers came to Ohio. Soon the people in Ohio—and the people in the 13 colonies—began to think of themselves as Americans.

"The king of England won't tell us what to do any more!" these people said. "We are going to make a new, free country!"

First settlement in Ohio

Northwest Territory
13 New States

In 1776 war broke out between the people in America and the English rulers. This was called the Revolutionary War (rev • oh • LOO • shun • airy wore). During this war George Washington ordered Fort Laurens (LOR • enz) to be built in Ohio. This was the westernmost fort built by the American army.

George Washington led the American army to victory. Ohio became part of a new country—the United States of America. But Ohio wasn't a state yet. Ohio became part of the large Northwest Territory. Some of the territory was reserved for those who had been there first—the Indians.

Settlers began to swarm into Ohio. Most of them floated down the Ohio River on flatboats. In the years 1788-1789, thousands of people came to live in Ohio.

The Indians were pushed from the land that had been reserved for them. The Indians began to fight back. Some Indians waited by the banks of the Ohio River and killed the new settlers. Indians also attacked the new towns.

Soldiers were sent to protect the settlers. But
Chief Little Turtle formed an army of Indians. They
killed hundreds of American soldiers. The settlers
were scared. They started to leave Ohio quicker than
they had come there. George Washington was
president of the United States at this time. He could
see that he had to do something.

President Washington sent "Mad" Anthony Wayne
to save the Ohio territory. General Wayne was

already an American hero because of his bravery
during the Revolutionary War. People called him
"Mad" because he took great risks. Wayne taught his
soldiers how to fight the Indians. Meanwhile, Chief
Little Turtle formed one of the biggest Indian armies
of all time.

In 1794 Anthony Wayne's soldiers beat the Indians
in a bloody fight, the Battle of Fallen Timbers.
Soon after this, there were no more Indian wars in
Ohio.

Replica of Ohio's first capitol

Ohio became the 17th state in 1803. Over 60,000 people lived in the new state. The first capital of Ohio was the town of Chillicothe (chill • ih • KOTH • ee). In 1816 Columbus (ko • LUM • bus) was made the capital.

Ohio is 230 miles across in its greatest distance from east to west. The longest part from north to south is 210 miles. Lake Erie is to the north. The Ohio River winds along the eastern and southern borders. Five states border Ohio. They are Michigan, Pennsylvania, West Virginia, Kentucky, and Indiana.

Paddle wheeler on Musk River

More and more people came to Ohio. Some took
steamboats down the Ohio River. In 1840 a
stagecoach road was completed. This was the
National Road. It went from Maryland to Illinois,
passing through the center of Ohio. In 1848 the first
of many railroads was built in Ohio. Ohio became
known as the "Gateway State" because it connected
East and West.

As the Civil War (SIV • il wore) neared, Ohio also
became the gateway for the "Underground
Railroad."

Once slaves escaped north of the Ohio River they were in the free state of Ohio. But a law said that escaped slaves had to be returned. Many Ohio people hated slavery. They helped slaves escape to Canada (CAN • ah • da), which had no law to return slaves. So the "Underground Railroad" wasn't really a railroad. And it wasn't underground. It was a series of houses and hiding places where slaves rested during their escape to Canada.

A view of Cleveland

After the Civil War, people came to the United States from many different countries. Many went to Ohio to work in the factories. Ohio's cities grew.

Cleveland (KLEEV • land) grew into the largest. Ships carried iron ore to Cleveland's steel mills. In 1870 the big Standard Oil Company was formed in Cleveland. And in 1879 Cleveland became the first American city to have electric street lights.

When Cleveland was first lit, people closed their eyes. They thought the lights would blind them. What

Left: Terminal Tower

Right: Ship in Cleveland's harbor

if they saw Cleveland now? The city sparkles with
light!

Cleveland is a fine place to begin a trip through
Ohio. It has more people than any Ohio city. With its
suburbs, Cleveland stretches for 50 miles along
Lake Erie. For a good view go to the top of Terminal
Tower. This big building has a railroad station in
its basement.

Night and day boats bring iron ore into the
harbor. The ore is made into steel in Cleveland's
mills. Cleveland is one of America's leading steel-
making cities. The steel goes into making cars, tools,
and airplanes for all of America.

Terminal Tower and other big buildings are in a downtown area called Public Square. A statue of Moses Cleaveland stands in the Square. Moses Cleaveland founded this city in 1796. According to one story, a newspaper printed the name wrong. That's why it is spelled C-l-e-v-e-l-a-n-d today.

You can have a lot of fun in Cleveland. At the Health Museum, you can see a giant model of your brain. The zoo and the aquarium (a • KWAR • ee • um) are in two beautiful parks. And don't miss the Cultural Gardens, which show how gardens look in different parts of the world.

The Cuyahoga (ky • HOAG • ah) River winds through Cleveland. This river was so polluted that it actually caught on fire in 1969. Now people are working to make Cleveland's water and air cleaner. The old buildings are also being torn down. Cleaner, safer buildings are being built.

Preparing "green" tires for the next curing stage in tire making

Earthmover tire change

Ohio is a great manufacturing state. That means many things are made here.

Akron (AK•run) is the biggest rubber-making city in the world. Long ago, rubber only came from trees. Now it can be *made* in factories. The tires on your car and the eraser on your pencil may have been made in Akron.

Refinery in Lima

Toledo Museum of Art

Toledo (toe • LEE • doe) is a big glass-making city. The windows in your house and the glasses you drink from may have come from Toledo.

Youngstown (YUNGS • town)—like Cleveland is one of the world's great steel-making cities. Your stove and your sink may have been made in Youngstown. What do you use to wash your hands? How do you weigh yourself? How was your house built? Soap, scales, and bricks are three more of Ohio's products.

You will remember that one of Ohio's nicknames is "Mother of Presidents." About 25 miles southeast of Akron is the city of Canton (CAN•tun). Visit McKinley Memorial, where William McKinley is buried. McKinley was born in Niles, Ohio. He was a school teacher, a soldier, and a lawyer in Canton. McKinley was the 25th president of the United States. In 1901 he was shaking hands in a crowd when a man shot him. President McKinley lived for nine days, but the doctors couldn't save him. The statue at McKinley Memorial shows how he looked as he made his last speech.

Throughout Ohio you can visit places where presidents lived. One of the most interesting is President Garfield's house. James Garfield was the last president who was born in a log cabin. The cabin has been rebuilt to look just as it did when James Garfield was a boy.

Top:
William Taft Home

Bottom:
Tomb of
James A. Garfield

Highway 40 leads into Columbus. Highway 40 is the old National Road. People traveled over it in stagecoaches. They stopped at inns to eat, drink, and rest. Some of the old inns are still here. Stop at one on your way to Columbus.

Columbus is the capital of Ohio. It is near the center of the state. Columbus is the largest city in the world named after Christopher Columbus. A statue of the explorer stands outside City Hall.

The Avenue of Flags is near City Hall Plaza. The flags of all 50 states fly over this street. Can you see *your* state flag?

Airplane and car parts are made in Columbus. It is also the main home of Ohio State University—one of the biggest schools in the world.

Left:
Pro Football Hall of
Fame, Canton

Top left:
Avenue of Flags,
Columbus

Top right:
Statue of Christopher
Columbus

Cincinnati (sin • sin • NAT • ee) lies on the banks of the Ohio River. Cincinnati is called the "Queen City," because it is so beautiful.

The Ohio River is important to this city. Boats on the river carry materials to and from Cincinnati. Go on an overnight ride on the *Delta Queen*, an old-time steamboat. A hundred years ago people went up and down the Ohio River in boats like the *Delta Queen*.

As you float along, remember that escaping slaves had to cross the Ohio River, often on rafts. Cincinnati was one of the main stopping places of the "Underground Railroad." You can visit houses where these slaves hid.

Playing cards and tools are made in Cincinnati. And the biggest soap factory in the world is here. They'll show you how soap is made, but they won't make you use it.

Skyline of Cincinnati
with Stadium in
foreground

Cities grew up along
the Ohio River

Rankin House, used by the
Underground Railroad

Top right: Polar bears at Cincinnati Zoo

Bottom right: Cincinnati Symphony Orchestra

Above: Seals at Cincinnati Zoo

Cincinnati is famous for its orchestra, opera, and museums. The city's zoo has the best group of big cats in the world. If the Cincinnati Reds are in town, go to the Riverfront Stadium to watch a game. The Reds are the oldest of all pro baseball teams. In 1869, their first pro year, the Reds won 64 games and lost none.

Left:
Eden Park, Refectory Pool

Top left:
Cuyahoga Valley

Top right:
Cuyahoga Valley

Ohio is known for its big cities. But it is also known for its natural beauty. About a fourth of Ohio is covered by forests. In Indian days, forests covered nearly all of Ohio. The nuts of one kind of tree reminded the Indians of the eye of a buck deer. This is why Ohio's official nickname is the ''Buckeye State.''

You'll enjoy Hueston (HYEW • stun) Woods. At this state park you can pick up fossils of plants and animals. Fossils are rocks that have the remains of living things. These plants and animals lived here millions of years ago when Ohio was covered by water.

Ohio is lovely when the apple trees blossom. A famous tree planter came to Ohio about 1800. He wore a sack for a shirt and no shoes. Wherever this man went he planted apple seeds.

"Johnny always comes back to take care of the young trees," people said. The man's name was John Chapman. But people called him "Johnny Appleseed."

Left:
Ash Cave in Hocking Hills State Park

Right:
Ohio apples ready for shipping

In the fall, there are apple festivals in many Ohio towns. The people dance and eat apples. They drink apple cider and make apple butter. And they remember the man who is supposed to have planted the first apple trees in Ohio—Johnny Appleseed.

The elk and buffalo are gone. But Ohio still has some of the wildlife that Johnny Appleseed saw in his travels. White-tailed deer, red foxes, woodchucks, bald eagles, and raccoons are a few of the animals. Catfish, bass, and perch are found in the state's rivers and lakes.

Most of Ohio's wealth comes from factories. But Ohio has a lot of fine farmland. Leading crops are corn, wheat, soybeans, apples, and grapes. Farmers also raise dairy cattle, beef cattle, hogs, and sheep.

Cuyahoga Valley

The ground itself is full of many treasures. Each year, millions of tons of coal are mined. The coal is used to heat houses and buildings. Ohio has enough salt to supply the whole world for many years. One salt mine goes *under* the city of Cleveland. Other important minerals are oil, natural gas, limestone, and sandstone.

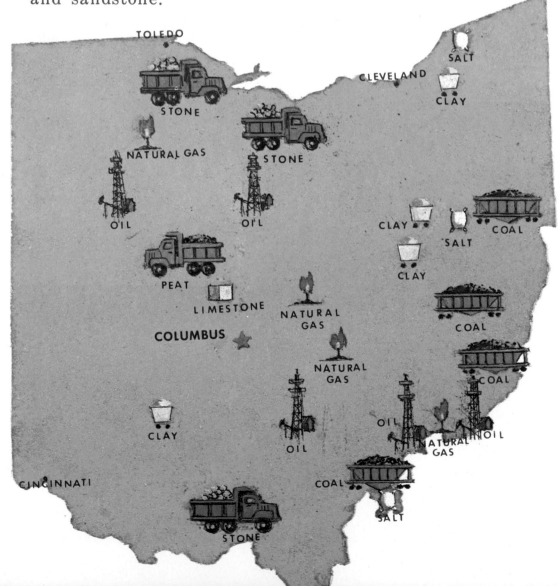

Visit the city of Dayton. Machinery and many other products are made in Dayton. The city has also been home to some of Ohio's most famous people.

A great poet, Paul Laurence Dunbar, was born in Dayton. Dunbar's parents had been slaves. The family was very poor. Paul wrote his first poems when he was seven years old. Later, he sold copies of his first book himself. Paul Laurence Dunbar wrote with feeling about Black people. You can visit his home, which is now a state memorial in Dayton.

Ohio has one more nickname—the "Mother of Inventors." The city of Dayton (DAY • tun) was home to some of those inventors.

Your great-grandfather had to crank his car to start it. Cranking was hard and dangerous. Charles Kettering of Dayton thought there had to be an easier way. He invented the "self-starter." Thanks to Charles Kettering, now you just have to turn a key to start a car.

In the early 1900's there were two brothers—Orville and Wilbur Wright. The Wright brothers owned a bicycle shop in Dayton. But they spent most of their time trying to build a machine that could fly.

"A flying machine? Don't those crazy Wright brothers know that only *birds* can fly?" people said.

Their first airplanes did not fly. But the Wright brothers kept on working and testing their airplanes—even though people came from miles around to laugh at them.

On December 17, 1903, the Wright brothers made the world's first airplane flight. It took place at Kitty Hawk, North Carolina. However, the brothers had done much of their work in Dayton. The next time you see a jumbo jet, remember "those crazy Wright brothers" who invented the airplane.

Today, the huge Wright-Patterson Air Force Base
is just outside Dayton. Visit the Air Force Museum
at the base. You can see World War I airplanes. You
can see missiles that have been sent into space.
And you can see one of the Wright brothers' early
airplanes.

Another very famous inventor was born in Ohio. He was Thomas Edison—often thought of as the greatest inventor of all time. Thomas Edison invented the electric light bulb. Thanks to him, your house can be as bright at midnight as it is at noon. Two of Edison's other inventions are the record player and the movie camera. People like to visit Thomas Edison's birthplace, in Milan (MY • lahn), Ohio.

Garrett Morgan, a black inventor, saw a girl hit by a car. He wanted to find a way to stop accidents like this. In 1923 he invented an automatic stop sign. Think about him the next time you see a stoplight.

Other inventions by Ohioans are the cash register and a process for making aluminum with electricity.

The Wright brothers would be proud of two modern Ohioans. John Glenn was born in Cambridge (CAME • brij), Ohio. He was the first American to orbit the Earth. John Glenn circled Earth three times in his 1962 space voyage.

Canoeing on Mohican River

Neil Armstrong was born in Wapakoneta
(waw • paw • ko • NET • ah), Ohio. He was the first
man to walk on the moon!

Mound Builders and astronauts ...

Presidents and inventors ...

Cities where rubber, steel, and glass
are made ...

Ohio really is—something great!

Facts About OHIO

Area—41,222 square miles
Highest Point—1,550 feet above sea level (Campbell Hill)
Lowest Point—433 feet above sea level (near the Ohio River)
Hottest Recorded Temperature—113° (in 1897, in Thurman; and in
                          1934, near Gallipolis)
Coldest Recorded Temperature—minus 39° (in 1899, in Milligan)
Statehood—17th state, March 1, 1803
Capital—Columbus (1816)
Other Captials—Chillicothe (1803-1810 and 1812-1815)
               Zanesville (1810-1812)
Counties—88
U.S. Senators—2
U.S. Representatives—21
Electoral Votes—23
State Senators—33
State Representatives—99
State Song—"Beautiful Ohio," by Ballard MacDonald and Mary Earl
State Motto—"With God, All Things Are Possible."
Nickname—Buckeye State (also called "Mother of Presidents,"
        "Mother of Inventors." and the "Gateway State.")
State Seal—Adopted in 1868
State Flag—Adopted in 1902
Principal Rivers—Ohio (flows for 450 miles along southern and
              southeast borders)
              Scioto (237 miles long)
              Muskingum
              Little Miami
              Cuyahoga
  (Ohio has a total of 44,000 miles of rivers and streams.)
Lakes—2500 within the state
State Symbols—Tree: Buckeye
            Flower: Scarlet carnation
            Gem stone: Flint
            Drink: Tomato juice
Farm Products—Corn, soybeans, wheat, oats, tomatoes, grapes,
            apples, beef cattle, dairy products, hogs, eggs, greenhouse
            products.
Fishing—Carp, catfish, yellow pike, yellow perch, white bass.
Mining—Coal, petroleum, salt, sandstone, limestone, clay.
Manufacturing Products—Machinery, chemicals, rubber products,
            glass products, plastic products, buses, truck bodies,
            trailers, iron, steel, food.

State Flag

State Seal

State Bird
(Cardinal)

State Flower
(Scarlet Carnation)

State Tree
(Buckeye)

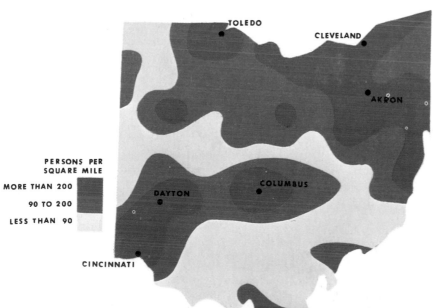

PERSONS PER
SQUARE MILE

MORE THAN 200

90 TO 200

LESS THAN 90

Population—10,797,419 (1980 census)

Major Cities— 1980 census

Cleveland	1,898,720
Columbus	1,093,293
Cincinnati	1,100,895
Toledo	656,940
Akron	660,328
Dayton	830,070
Youngstown-Warren	531,350

45

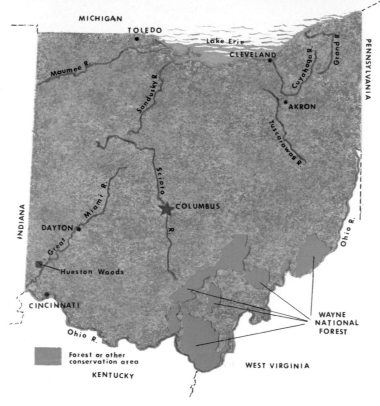

Ohio History

1669-1670—La Salle explores area for France

1750—English explorers, led by Christopher Gist, go to Ohio

1754-1763—England and France fight over Ohio and other lands
         in America (known as the French and Indian War)

1763—England becomes the ruling country in Ohio.

1787—Northwest Territory established in new country—United States of America

1788—Marietta becomes first permanent settlement in Ohio

1788—Cincinnati founded

1791—Indians, led by Chief Little Turtle, kill hundreds of
         American settlers in Ohio

1794—"Mad" Anthony Wayne defeats Little Turtle in Battle of
         Fallen Timbers

1795—Treaty of Green Ville puts an end to Indian Wars

1796—Cleveland founded by Moses Cleaveland

1800—Ohio becomes a separate territory

1803—Ohio becomes the 17th state on March 1; Chillicothe is capital

1804—Coonskin Library opened at Amesville

1811—First steamboat on Ohio River, *New Orleans,* goes from Pittsburgh
         to Cincinnati

1816—Columbus becomes state capital

1817—Governor Worthington establishes Ohio State Library in Columbus

1825—Public school system begun

1831—James A. Garfield born in log cabin in Orange

1833—Oberlin College founded, first college in U.S. for both men and women

1840—National Road completed

1861—Civil War begins; over 345,000 Ohio men fight in Northern army

1865—Civil War ends

1868—Ulysses S. Grant elected 18th president of U.S.

1869—Cincinnati Reds become first pro baseball team

1870—Standard Oil Company organized in Cleveland

1872—Poet Paul Laurence Dunbar is born in Dayton

1877—Rutherford B. Hayes becomes 19th president of U.S.

1879—Cash register invented by James Ritty of Dayton

1880—James A. Garfield elected 20th president of U.S.; this makes three presidents in a row who were born in Ohio

1888—Benjamin Harrison elected 23rd president

1896—William McKinley elected 25th president

1901—President McKinley is assassinated

1901—Wright brothers build wind tunnel for testing airplanes in Dayton

1903—Ohio celebrates its 100th birthday as a state

1906—Paul Laurence Dunbar dies

1908—William H. Taft elected 27th president

1909—Charles Kettering of Dayton invents the self-starter for cars

1913—Floods in Ohio kill five hundred people

1914—Ohio begins construction of dams in flood control project

1917—U.S. enters World War I; 200,000 Ohio men in uniform

1920—Warren G. Harding elected 29th president; he is the 7th president from Ohio

1923—Garrett Morgan, a black inventor, invents the automatic stop sign

1937—Great floods in Ohio, but dams save many lives

1941—U.S. enters World War II; over 800,000 Ohio men and women in uniform

1955—Ohio Turnpike opened

1959—Terms of governor and other state officials are increased from two years to four

1962—John Glenn of Cambridge is first American to orbit Earth

1963—Ohio begins a new program to attract more industry

1964—Jerrie Mock is the first woman pilot to make a solo flight around the world in a single engine plane

1967—Carl Stokes elected mayor of Cleveland; first Black mayor of a big U.S. city

1969—Neil Armstrong of Wapakoneta is the first person to walk on the moon

1971—Ohio begins a state income tax

1974—Former astronaut, John Glenn is elected to the U.S. Senate

1979—Nuclear power station opens at Moscow on the Ohio River

INDEX

About the Author:

Dennis Fradin attended Northwestern University on a creative writing scholarship and graduated in 1967. While still at Northwestern, he published his first stories in *Ingenue* magazine and also won a prize in *Seventeen's* short story competition. A prolific writer, Dennis Fradin has been regularly publishing stories in such diverse places as *The Saturday Evening Post, Scholastic, National Humane Review, Midwest,* and *The Teaching Paper.* He has also scripted several educational films. Since 1970 he has taught second grade reading in a Chicago school—a rewarding job, which, the author says, "provides a captive audience on whom I test my children's stories." Married and the father of two children, Dennis Fradin spends his free time with his family or playing a myriad of sports and games with his childhood chums.

About the Artist:

Robert Ulm, a Chicago resident, has been an advertising and editorial artist in both New York and Chicago. Mr. Ulm is a successful painter as well as an illustrator. In his spare time he enjoys fishing and playing tennis.